How to Start a Successful Online Business:

A Step-by-Step Guide for Entrepreneurs

ROBERT JAY SAKI

Copyright © [Robert Jay Saki] [2024]

All rights reserved. No part of this publication may be reproduced, distributed, or transmitted in any form or by any means, including photocopying, recording, or other electronic or mechanical methods, without the prior written permission of the publisher, except in the case of brief quotations embodied in critical reviews and certain other noncommercial uses permitted by copyright law.

TABLE OF CONTENTS

Appendix: Resources and Tools for Online Entrepreneurs

- Website and E-commerce Platform Recommendations

Chapter 1: Introduction

1.1 Why Start an Online Business.

Starting a successful online business has become an increasingly popular and lucrative venture for entrepreneurs in today's digital age. With the rise of technology and the accessibility of the internet, the possibilities for creating a thriving online business are endless. However, navigating the complex world of e-commerce can be daunting, especially for those new to the online business landscape.

This book, "How to Start a Successful Online Business: A Step-by-Step Guide for Entrepreneurs," is designed to provide aspiring online business owners with the knowledge, tools, and strategies needed to launch and grow their ventures successfully. Whether you are starting from scratch or looking to take your existing brick-and-mortar business online, this comprehensive guide will walk you through each essential step, helping you avoid common pitfalls and maximize your chances of success.

In this book, we will cover everything from finding your niche and building a compelling brand to setting up your online store, driving traffic to your website, and providing outstanding customer service.

We will delve into effective marketing techniques, such as search engine optimization (SEO), social media marketing, and email marketing, to help you reach your target audience and strengthen your online presence.

Additionally, legal and financial considerations, as well as data analysis and scalability, will be addressed to ensure you are well-informed and prepared to handle the various aspects of running an online business. We will also emphasize the importance of continual learning and innovation in order to stay ahead of the competition and adapt to a rapidly evolving digital marketplace.

Throughout this guide, you will find practical tips, real-life examples, and actionable steps that can be implemented immediately. Whether you are a solo entrepreneur or looking to build a team, this book is for anyone who is passionate about building a successful online business.

Though the journey of starting an online business may have its challenges, it also presents incredible opportunities for growth and success. With the right mindset, dedication, and the knowledge shared in this book, you will be well-equipped to embark on your entrepreneurial journey and achieve your online business goals.

So, if you are ready to turn your dreams into reality and embark on a path to entrepreneurial success, let's dive into the step-by-step guide that will empower you to build and grow a thriving online business.

1.2 Benefits of Starting an Online Business

Starting an online business offers numerous advantages that can make it an appealing option for entrepreneurs. Here are some key benefits:

1. Low startup costs: Compared to traditional brick-and-mortar businesses, starting an online business typically requires lower initial investment. You can avoid expenses such as renting physical space, buying inventory, or hiring staff, which significantly reduces your overhead costs.

2. Flexibility and convenience: Online businesses offer the advantage of flexibility and convenience. You have the freedom to work from anywhere with an internet connection, allowing you to create a schedule that suits your lifestyle.

This flexibility is particularly beneficial for those who want to balance work with personal commitments or travel.

3. Global reach: With an online business, you have access to a global market. The internet transcends geographical boundaries, enabling you to reach customers from all over the world. You can expand your customer base beyond local limitations and tap into untapped markets, increasing your potential for growth and profitability.

4. 24/7 availability: Unlike traditional businesses with fixed operating hours, an online business operates 24/7. Your website can accept orders, provide information, and engage with customers at any time, allowing you to generate revenue even while you sleep. This constant availability ensures that you never miss out on potential sales and opportunities.

5. **Cost-effective marketing options:** Online marketing offers a range of cost-effective strategies to promote your business. From social media marketing and search engine optimization to email marketing and content creation, digital marketing channels allow you to effectively reach your target

audience without breaking the bank. This makes it easier for small businesses to compete with larger competitors.

6. Access to valuable data and insights: Online businesses have the advantage of collecting and analyzing a wealth of data. This data can provide valuable insights into customer behavior, preferences, and purchasing patterns. By leveraging this information, you can make data-driven decisions, optimize your marketing strategies, and improve your overall business performance.

7. Scalability and growth potential: Compared to traditional businesses, online businesses have higher scalability and growth potential. With the right strategies and systems in place, you can easily scale your operations to accommodate increased customers and sales. You can expand your product offerings, target new markets, and even automate processes to handle higher volumes.

8. Increased customer engagement: An online business allows for enhanced customer engagement and interaction. Through social media platforms, live chats, customer reviews, and personalized email campaigns, you can build strong relationships with your customers. This fosters trust and loyalty, leading to repeat purchases, positive word-of-mouth, and a strong brand reputation.

Overall, starting an online business offers a range of benefits, including low startup costs, flexibility, global reach, 24/7 availability, cost-effective marketing options, access to valuable data, scalability, and increased customer engagement. These advantages make it an attractive option for entrepreneurs seeking to start and grow a successful business in the digital age.

1.3 Key Considerations for Online Entrepreneurs

1. Research your market: Before starting an online business, it is crucial to thoroughly research your target market. Understand their needs, preferences, and buying behaviors to identify potential opportunities and gaps in the market.

2. Choose a profitable niche: Selecting the right niche is vital for the success of your online business. Look for niches that have high demand but relatively low competition. This will give you a better chance of capturing a significant share of the market.

3. Develop a unique value proposition: Differentiate your online business by developing a unique value proposition. Clearly articulate what sets your products or services apart from competitors and why customers should choose you.

4. Understand online consumer behavior: Online consumer behavior can be different from traditional brick-and-mortar settings. Educate yourself on the preferences, habits, and expectations of online shoppers to tailor your business strategies accordingly.

5. Build a professional website: Your website is the face of your online business. Invest in creating a professional, user-friendly website that showcases your brand and products/services effectively. Ensure it is mobile-responsive and optimized for search engines.

6. Leverage digital marketing strategies: Effective online marketing is essential for driving traffic and generating sales. Familiarize yourself with various digital marketing techniques such as search engine optimization (SEO), social media marketing, email marketing, and pay-per-click (PPC) advertising. Develop a comprehensive digital marketing strategy to reach and engage your target audience.

7. Provide excellent customer service: Online businesses must prioritize providing exceptional customer service. Establish multiple channels for customer support, respond promptly to inquiries and issues, and strive to exceed customer expectations. Positive customer experiences can lead to repeat business and referrals.

8. Analyze data and make data-driven decisions: Collect and analyze data related to your online business performance to gain insights into buyer behavior, sales trends, and marketing strategies. Use this information to make informed decisions and continually optimize your business operations.

9. Consider legal and financial regulations: Online entrepreneurs must comply with legal and financial obligations specific to e-commerce. Research and understand regulations related to business registration, licenses, taxes, and intellectual property protection to ensure you are operating legally and ethically.

10. Stay adaptable and innovative: The digital landscape is constantly evolving, so it is essential for online entrepreneurs to stay adaptable and embrace change. Continuously educate yourself, stay updated with industry trends, and be open to adopting new technologies and strategies to remain competitive.

By considering these key factors, online entrepreneurs can position themselves for success and maximize their chances of building and scaling a successful online business.

Chapter 2: Finding Your Niche

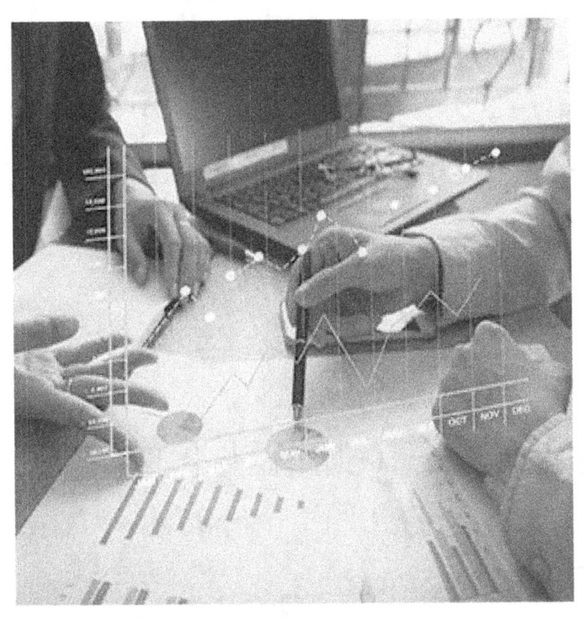

2.1 Defining Your Target Market

Defining your target market is the process of identifying and understanding the specific group of people or customers that your online business aims to serve. By clearly defining your target market, you can tailor your marketing strategies, product offerings, and overall business approach to best meet the needs and preferences of your ideal customers.

To define your target market, you should consider the following factors:

1. **Demographics:** This includes age, gender, location, income level, education, and other relevant characteristics. Understanding the demographics of your target market helps you create targeted marketing campaigns

and effectively communicate with your audience.

2. Psychographics: This refers to the psychological and behavioral traits of your target market. Consider their values, attitudes, interests, lifestyle choices, and purchasing behaviors. This understanding allows you to develop products and marketing messages that resonate with your audience.

3. Needs and Pain Points: Identify the specific needs, challenges, or problems your target market faces. By understanding their pain points, you can develop products or services that provide solutions and address their concerns.

4. **Competition Analysis:** Research your competitors and analyze their target market. Identify any gaps or unmet needs in the market that you can focus on and differentiate yourself from competitors.

5. **Customer Feedback and Insights:** Gather feedback from existing customers or conduct surveys to gain insights into their preferences, satisfaction levels, and areas for improvement. This feedback can help you refine your target market and make

necessary adjustments to better serve your customers.

When defining your target market, remember that it should be a specific and well-defined group. Trying to appeal to everyone can dilute your marketing efforts and make it difficult to differentiate your business. By honing in on a specific target market, you can develop a focused and effective marketing strategy that resonates with your ideal customers.

Regularly reassessing and refining your target market is

also important as consumer preferences and market dynamics change over time. Stay updated with industry trends and feedback from your customers to ensure your target market definition remains relevant and aligned with your business goals.

2.2 Identifying Profitable Niches

Identifying profitable niches involves finding specific market segments that have high demand and low competition, allowing you to target a specific audience and differentiate yourself from competitors. Here are some steps to help you identify profitable niches:

1. Research Market Trends: Stay updated on current market trends and consumer preferences. Look for emerging industries or sectors that have growing demand but limited competition.

2. Identify Customer Pain Points: Pay attention to common problems or challenges that customers are facing within a particular industry or market. Find ways to address these pain points with your products or services.

3. Assess Competition: Conduct a competitive analysis to understand the landscape within your potential niche. Evaluate the number of competitors and the quality of their offerings. Look for gaps or areas where you can offer something unique and valuable.

4. Consider Target Audience: Define your ideal customer profile and understand their needs, desires, and preferences. Look for underserved or overlooked segments within the larger market that you can cater to effectively.

5. Explore Niche Communities: Engage with online communities, forums, and social media groups related to your potential niche. Listen to conversations, ask questions, and gain insights into the challenges, interests, and desires of the community members.

6. Conduct Keyword Research: Use keyword research tools to identify relevant keywords and search terms that indicate high demand within your potential niche. Look for keywords with a decent search volume and relatively low competition.

7. Analyze Profitability: Consider the potential profitability of your niche by evaluating factors such as average pricing, profit margins, and customer lifetime value. Assess if the niche has the potential to generate sustainable revenue and profitability.

8. Validate Your Idea: Before fully committing to a niche, test the market by conducting surveys, running small-scale experiments, or creating a minimum viable product (MVP) to gauge interest and gather feedback from potential customers.

By following these steps, you can identify profitable niches that align with your interests, expertise, and market opportunities, setting the foundation for a successful online business.

Additional resources you can consult for more guidance on identifying profitable niches include market research reports, industry publications, and business blogs. Additionally, seeking advice from industry experts or consulting with a business mentor can provide valuable insights and guidance throughout the process.

2.3 Conducting Market Research

Conducting market research is a crucial step in understanding your target market, customer needs, and competitive landscape. It helps you gather data and insights to make informed business decisions. Here are the key steps involved in conducting market research:

1. **Define your Research Objectives:** Clearly articulate what you want to learn from your market research. Identify the specific questions or

problems you aim to address, such as understanding customer preferences, assessing market size, or evaluating the competition.

2. Determine your Research Methodology: Choose the most appropriate research methods based on your objectives and available resources. Some common research methods include surveys, interviews, focus groups, observational studies, and secondary research (using existing data and reports).

3. Identify your Target Audience: Define the specific demographic, psychographic, and behavioral characteristics of your target market. This will help you recruit representative participants for your research and ensure your findings are applicable to your target audience.

4. Conduct Primary Research: Primary research involves collecting original data directly from your target audience. This can be done through surveys or interviews. Design questionnaires or discussion guides that align with your research objectives and ensure that your questions are unbiased and focused.

5. Analyze Data: Once you've collected your primary research data, analyze it to identify patterns, trends, and insights. Use software or tools to process and organize the data effectively. Look for recurring themes and examine the data from different angles to gain a comprehensive understanding of your target market.

6. Conduct Secondary Research: Supplement your primary research findings with secondary research, which involves analyzing existing data and reports relevant to your industry, market, and competitors. This can include industry reports, government statistics, market research studies, and competitor analyses. Capture key industry trends, market size, growth rates, and customer segments to inform your decision-making.

7. Evaluate the Competitive Landscape: Assess your competitors, their offerings, pricing, marketing strategies, and customer reviews. Identify their strengths, weaknesses, and positioning in the market. This will help you identify opportunities for differentiation and competitive advantage.

8. Interpret and Apply Findings: Translate your research findings into actionable insights. Use the data and insights to refine your business strategy, optimize your marketing efforts, and make informed decisions regarding your target audience, product development, pricing, and positioning.

Market research is an ongoing process and should be revisited periodically to stay updated with evolving customer needs and market trends. By conducting thorough market research, you can better understand your target market and make informed decisions that will contribute to the success of your online business.

Chapter 3: Building Your Brand

3.1 Developing a Unique Value Proposition

Developing a unique value proposition is crucial for any business, especially online businesses. It is a concise statement that clearly communicates the unique benefits and value that your products or services offer to your target audience. It sets you apart from your competitors and helps you attract and retain customers.

To develop a unique value proposition, you need to consider the following steps:

1. Understand Your Target Market: Research and understand your target audience's needs, preferences, and pain points. Identify what they value the most and what problems or challenges they are facing.

2. Identify Your Key Differentiators: Identify what sets your business apart from your competitors. This could be a unique feature, a specific expertise, a different pricing strategy, exceptional customer service, or a specific niche market you're targeting.

3. Determine the Benefits: Determine the specific benefits your products or services offer to your customers. How will they solve their problems or improve their lives? Focus on the value that your offerings bring to your customers.

4. Craft a Clear and Compelling Statement: Use the information gathered in the previous steps to create a concise and compelling value proposition. Avoid jargon or complex language and keep it simple and easy to understand. It should be clear, specific, and memorable.

5. Test and Refine: Test and validate your value proposition with your target audience. Seek feedback and gather data to refine and improve your value proposition based on customer responses. Continuously evaluate and update your value proposition as your business evolves and customer needs change.

Remember, a strong and unique value proposition will help you differentiate your business, attract customers, and build long-term relationships. It should clearly communicate the benefits and value you offer, addressing the needs and desires of your target audience.

Here are some additional tips to help you develop a strong value proposition:

1. **Be Specific:** Avoid generic statements and vague claims.

Instead, be specific about what makes your products or services unique and better than your competitors'. Focus on the specific outcomes or solutions you provide.

2. Highlight Your Competitive Advantage: Clearly articulate what sets you apart from your competitors. This could be a unique feature, superior quality, faster delivery, exceptional customer service, or a combination of factors that makes your business stand out.

3. Focus on the Customer: Your value proposition should be customer-centric and focus on addressing their pain points or desires. Highlight how your products or services improve their lives or solve their problems. Use customer testimonials or case studies to add credibility and demonstrate real-world impact.

4. Be Clear and Concise: Keep your value proposition simple, clear, and easy to understand. Avoid technical jargon or complex language that may confuse your audience. Use straightforward language that resonates with your target market.

5. Continuously Test and Refine: Your value proposition should be an iterative process. Continuously gather feedback from your customers and prospects to understand what resonates with them and what could be improved. Use A/B testing, surveys, and customer interviews to gather insights and refine your value proposition accordingly.

6. Align with Your Brand and Messaging: Ensure that your value proposition is aligned with your brand identity and overall messaging. It should reflect your brand's values, tone, and style. Consistency across all marketing channels and touchpoints will help build a strong and cohesive brand image.

7. Monitor Your Competition:

Keep a close eye on your competitors and their value propositions. Identify any gaps or areas where you can differentiate yourself further. By understanding what your competitors are offering, you can position your business uniquely.

8. Communicate Clear Benefits:

Your value proposition should clearly communicate the benefits that customers can expect from choosing your products or services. Be specific and highlight the value that your offerings provide. Whether it's cost savings, time efficiency, improved productivity, or enhanced quality, focus on the tangible benefits that resonate with your target audience.

9. Differentiate from Competitors: Your value proposition should emphasize what makes your business unique and different from your competitors. Identify your key advantages, such as proprietary technology, a unique business model, exceptional customer service, or an exclusive partnership. Highlighting these differentiators will help you stand out in a crowded market.

10. Emphasize the Emotional Appeal: In addition to rational benefits, consider incorporating an emotional appeal into your value proposition. Appeal to your customers' desires, aspirations, or emotions. For example, if you sell fitness products, your value proposition could emphasize the feeling of confidence and well-being that comes with being fit.

11. Make it Memorable: Craft your value proposition in a way that is memorable and easily recognizable. Use concise and impactful language that conveys your unique value in a compelling manner. A memorable value proposition will help your business stick in the minds of potential customers and distinguish you from competitors.

12. Align with Customer Feedback: Listen to your customers and incorporate their feedback into your value proposition. Pay attention to the pain points they share, their preferences, and their perceptions of your business. By aligning your value proposition with the needs and feedback of your customers, you can ensure that it resonates and addresses their specific concerns.

Developing a unique value proposition is an ongoing process that requires continuous refinement and adaptation to stay relevant in a dynamic business environment. Regularly review and evaluate the effectiveness of your value proposition and make adjustments based on customer feedback, market trends, and industry developments. A well-crafted and compelling value proposition will not only attract customers but also create a strong foundation for the success of your online business.

3.2 Creating a Memorable Brand Identity

Creating a memorable brand identity involves developing a unique and recognizable image that sets your online business apart from competitors and leaves a lasting impression on your target audience. Here are some key elements to consider when building your brand identity:

1. Define your brand values: Determine the core values and beliefs that your business stands for. This will shape the overall personality and messaging of your brand.

2. Develop a brand personality: Think of your brand as a person and give it distinct characteristics and traits. Consider how you want your brand to be perceived by customers - friendly, professional, innovative, etc.

3. Design a visually appealing logo: Your logo is the visual representation of your brand and should be easily recognizable. Work with a professional designer to create a visually appealing and memorable logo that reflects your brand's personality.

4. Choose a consistent color scheme and typography: Consistency in your visual elements is crucial for brand recognition. Select a color palette and font styles that align with your brand's tone and maintain consistency across all brand assets.

5. Craft a compelling brand story: A powerful narrative can engage customers and create an emotional connection to your brand. Share the story of how your business started, its mission, and how it adds value to customers' lives.

6. Establish brand guidelines: Create a brand style guide that outlines the proper usage of your visual elements, such as logo placement, color usage, and typography. This ensures consistency across all marketing materials and reinforces brand recognition.

7. Use consistent messaging: Develop a unique brand voice and tone that aligns with your target audience and reflects your brand personality. Consistently apply this voice in all communications, including website content, social media posts, and customer interactions.

8. Create memorable brand experiences: Look for opportunities to engage with your audience in ways that create a lasting impression. This could include personalized packaging, unique unboxing experiences, or hosting special events or promotions that align with your brand values.

9. Build strong brand associations: Collaborate with influencers or brand ambassadors who align with your brand values and have a similar target audience. Leveraging their influence can help reinforce brand associations and increase brand visibility.

10. Engage with your audience: Be proactive in building relationships with your customers. Respond to inquiries and feedback promptly, offer exceptional customer service, and consistently deliver on your brand promise.

Remember, creating a memorable brand identity is an ongoing process. Continuously monitor your brand's perception and adapt your strategies accordingly to ensure your brand remains relevant and resonates with your target audience.

3.3 Building a Professional Website

A professional website is crucial for the success of your online business. It serves as the online storefront where customers can learn about your brand, explore your products or services, and make purchases. Building a professional website involves several key considerations:

1. User-Friendly Design: The design of your website should be clean, visually appealing, and easy to navigate. It should have a clear and logical layout, with intuitive menus and navigation bars. Ensure that it is mobile-friendly, as a growing number of consumers browse the internet on their smartphones and tablets.

2. Brand Consistency: Your website should reflect your brand identity and maintain consistency with other marketing materials. Use consistent color schemes, fonts, and graphics to reinforce your brand image. Incorporate your logo and tagline prominently to enhance brand recognition.

3. Compelling Content: Your website should have high-quality, well-written content that engages visitors and persuades them to take action. Craft compelling product descriptions, informative blog posts, and clear calls-to-action that guide users towards making a purchase or contacting you for more information.

4. Secure Checkout Process: Implement secure payment systems to protect customer information and build trust. Ensure that your website has an SSL certificate to encrypt data and provide a secure browsing experience. Display trust badges or logos of trusted payment providers to reassure customers about the security of their transactions.

5. Search Engine Optimization (SEO): Optimize your website's content and structure to improve its visibility in search engine results. Conduct keyword research to identify relevant and high-ranking keywords for your business. Incorporate these keywords naturally into your website's content, meta tags, and URLs. Ensure that your website has a sitemap and is easily crawlable by search engines.

6. Fast Loading Speed: A slow-loading website can lead to high bounce rates and lost sales. Optimize your website's loading speed by compressing images, minimizing code, and leveraging caching techniques. Test your website's speed on different devices and browsers to ensure optimal performance.

7. **Analytics and Tracking:** Set up website analytics tools, such as Google Analytics, to track user behavior and gather valuable insights. Monitor metrics such as page views, conversion rates, and bounce rates to assess the effectiveness of your website and make data-driven decisions for improvements.

8. **Responsive Customer Support:** Provide accessible and responsive customer support

options on your website. Include contact information, such as phone numbers, email addresses, or live chat, so customers can easily reach out with inquiries or issues.

By considering these factors and implementing them in the design and development of your website, you can create a professional and user-friendly online platform that effectively represents your brand, engages customers, and generates sales.

Additionally, it is worth mentioning that there are various tools and resources that can assist you in building a professional website. These include website builders such as WordPress, Wix, Shopify, or Squarespace, which provide user-friendly interfaces and customizable templates. You can also hire a professional web designer or developer to create a custom website tailored to your specific needs and brand identity.

Remember that building a professional website is an ongoing process. Regularly update and optimize your content, monitor analytics, and stay up-to-date with the latest web design trends and technologies to ensure that your website remains effective and competitive in the ever-evolving online business landscape.

Chapter 4: Setting Up Your Online Store

4.1 Choosing the Right E-commerce Platform

Choosing the right e-commerce platform is a crucial decision for any online business. The e-commerce platform is the software or technology that provides the necessary infrastructure and tools to manage and operate an online store. Here are some factors to consider when selecting the right e-commerce platform for your business:

1. **Functionality:** Evaluate the platform's features and determine if they align with your business requirements. Key functionalities to look for include inventory management, product catalog, order management,

payment integration, shipping options, and customization capabilities.

2. Ease of use: Consider the platform's user interface and how user-friendly it is. Look for a platform that allows you to easily navigate and manage your store without requiring extensive technical knowledge.

3. Scalability: Assess whether the platform can accommodate the growth of your business. It should be able to handle increased traffic, sales, and product catalog expansion without compromising performance or requiring significant upgrades.

4. Integration options: Check if the platform integrates seamlessly with other essential business tools, such as accounting software, email marketing platforms, customer relationship management (CRM) systems, and analytics tools. Integration capabilities simplify data sharing and streamline your business operations.

5. Payment gateways: Ensure that the platform supports a wide range of secure, reliable, and convenient payment gateways. Consider the fees associated with each payment gateway and whether they align with your budget.

6. Mobile responsiveness: With the growing number of mobile shoppers, it is essential for your e-commerce platform to have mobile-responsive design and functionality. This ensures that your website is accessible and user-friendly on mobile devices.

7. Security: Look for a platform that prioritizes security. It should offer SSL certificates, secure checkout options, and other measures to protect customer data and ensure safe transactions.

8. Customer support: Consider the level of customer support provided by the platform. Look for easy access to technical support, resources, and documentation to assist you in managing your online store effectively.

9. Pricing: Evaluate the platform's pricing structure and determine if it aligns with your budget. Some platforms charge monthly fees, while others have transaction-based pricing models or a combination of both. Take into account any additional costs such as themes, add-ons, and upgrades.

10. Reviews and reputation: Research and read reviews about the platform to gauge its reputation and performance. Look for feedback from other users and consider their experiences before making a final decision.

By carefully considering these factors, you can choose the right e-commerce platform that best suits your business needs and supports your online store's growth and success.

Some popular e-commerce platforms to consider include Shopify, WooCommerce, Magento, BigCommerce, and Squarespace, among others. Research and compare the features and offerings of each platform to determine which one aligns best with your business requirements.

4.2 Optimizing Your Product Catalog

Once you have chosen the right e-commerce platform for your online business, it's important to optimize your product catalog to attract and convert customers. Here are some key considerations:

1. High-quality product images: Use professional-quality images that showcase your products in the best possible light. Ensure that the images are clear, properly sized, and visually appealing. Multiple images from different angles or with zoom options can also enhance the shopping experience.

2. Detailed and accurate product descriptions: Write informative and engaging product descriptions that provide all the necessary details about each item. Be specific about features, dimensions, materials, and any other relevant information that helps customers make informed purchasing decisions.

3. Organize products into categories and subcategories: Create a logical and user-friendly structure for your product catalog. Categorize products into relevant categories and subcategories to make it easier for customers to navigate and find what they are looking for.

4. Implement effective search and filtering options: A robust search function with filters enables customers to quickly and easily find products based on their specific criteria. Implement filters such as price range, color, size, brand, and other relevant attributes to make the shopping experience more efficient.

5. Product reviews and ratings: Allow customers to leave reviews and ratings for products they have purchased. This social proof can help build trust and credibility for your brand.

Displaying reviews and ratings can also assist potential customers in making purchasing decisions.

6. Cross-sell and upsell opportunities: Take advantage of cross-selling and upselling techniques by suggesting related or complementary products to customers. This can increase the average order value and boost overall sales.

7. Mobile optimization: With the increasing use of mobile devices for online shopping, it's crucial to ensure that your product catalog is fully optimized for mobile users. Responsive design, easy navigation, and seamless checkout processes are essential for a positive mobile shopping experience.

8. Inventory management: Implement a robust inventory management system to keep track of stock levels, monitor product availability, and automate reordering processes. This ensures that your product catalog is always up to date and avoids disappointing customers due to out-of-stock items.

By optimizing your product catalog, you can enhance the overall shopping experience for your customers, increase conversions, and drive sales for your online business.

4.3 Implementing Secure Payment Systems

When setting up your online store, it's crucial to implement secure payment systems to protect your customers' sensitive information and ensure a smooth and trustworthy transaction process. Here are some key considerations:

1. **Choose trusted payment gateways:** Select reputable payment gateway providers that are known for their security measures and reliability. Some popular options include PayPal, Stripe, Square, and Authorize.Net. Research the features, fees, and compatibility of each payment gateway to find the best fit for your business.

2. **Use SSL encryption:** Install and configure an SSL (Secure Sockets Layer) certificate on your website. This creates a secure connection between your customers' browsers and your

server, encrypting all sensitive data during transmission. Having an SSL certificate is essential for safeguarding customer information, building trust, and improving your website's search engine rankings.

3. **PCI compliance:** Ensure that your online store is fully compliant with the Payment Card Industry Data Security Standard (PCI DSS). This set of security standards is designed to protect cardholder data and prevent fraud. Work with your payment gateway provider and web host to ensure that your online store meets all PCI compliance requirements.

4. Implement fraud prevention measures: Use fraud prevention tools and techniques to minimize the risk of fraudulent transactions and chargebacks. This can include address verification systems (AVS), card verification value (CVV) checks, and fraud detection services. Regularly monitor transactions and implement measures to identify and prevent suspicious activity.

5. Secure customer data storage: Implement strong security measures to protect customer data stored on your website or server. This includes encrypting customer information, regularly updating and patching your website's software, and using strong passwords and access controls.

6. Communicate security measures to your customers: Assure your customers that their payment information is secure by prominently displaying trust badges, security seals, and SSL certificates on your website. Clearly explain your security measures and privacy policy to build trust and confidence with your customers.

7. Regularly update and test your systems: Stay vigilant and keep your payment systems up to date with the latest security patches and updates. Regularly conduct security audits and penetration tests to identify vulnerabilities and address them promptly.

By implementing secure payment systems, you not only protect your customers' sensitive information but also enhance their trust in your business. This can lead to increased sales and customer satisfaction, ultimately contributing to the success of your online business.

Chapter 5: Creating Compelling Content

5.1 Crafting Engaging Product Descriptions

Compelling product descriptions play a crucial role in captivating your audience and convincing them to make a purchase. Here are some tips to help you craft engaging product descriptions:

1. Understand your target audience: Before writing product descriptions, have a clear understanding of your target market and their preferences. Consider their needs, interests, and pain points, and tailor your descriptions accordingly.

2. Highlight benefits and solutions: Instead of focusing solely on product features, emphasize the benefits your product offers and the solutions it provides to customers' problems. Explain how your product can improve their lives, save them time or money, or address specific pain points.

3. Use persuasive language: Grab your readers' attention by using persuasive language and powerful adjectives. Create a sense of urgency or exclusivity by using words like "limited edition," "exclusive offer," or "highly sought after."

4. Tell a story: Engage your customers by telling a story behind your product. Share the inspiration, the story of its creation, or the problem it solves. Storytelling adds depth and emotion, making your product more relatable and memorable.

5. Keep it concise and scannable: Most online shoppers skim through product descriptions, so keep them concise and easy to scan. Use bullet points, subheadings, and short paragraphs to break up the text and make it more digestible.

6. Use descriptive and specific language: Instead of using vague and generic phrases, be specific and descriptive in your product descriptions. Provide measurements, materials, colors, and any other relevant details that can help customers make an informed decision.

7. **Include social proof:** Incorporate customer testimonials, reviews, or ratings to build trust and credibility. Showcasing positive experiences from other customers can help potential buyers feel more confident in their purchase.

8. **Encourage engagement and interaction:** Include a call-to-action in your product descriptions to prompt readers to take the desired action, such

as adding the item to their cart or contacting your customer support for more information.

9. Optimize for SEO: Incorporate relevant keywords in your product descriptions to improve the chances of your products appearing in search engine results. Conduct keyword research to identify the most relevant and high-traffic terms for your niche.

10. Test and iterate: Continuously monitor the performance of your product descriptions and make adjustments based on data and customer feedback. Test different formats, language styles, and approaches to optimize and improve your descriptions over time.

Remember, your product descriptions should not only inform but also inspire and create an emotional connection with your customers. By crafting engaging and persuasive product descriptions, you can enhance your chances of driving conversions and increasing sales.

5.2 Designing Attention-Grabbing Visuals

Designing attention-grabbing visuals refers to creating visually appealing and engaging graphics, images, and videos that capture the attention of your target audience. This is an important aspect of building your brand and attracting customers to your online business.

Here are some key points to consider when designing attention-grabbing visuals:

1. Consistency with your brand: Your visuals should align with your brand's identity and values.

Use colors, fonts, and imagery that are consistent with your brand's style and voice.

2. High-quality images and videos: Use high-resolution and professional-looking images and videos that are visually pleasing and showcase your products or services effectively.

3. Compelling product photography: Properly photograph your products to highlight their unique features and benefits. Use different angles, props, and lighting techniques to make your products visually appealing.

4. Infographics: Use infographics to present complex information or data in a visually appealing and easy-to-understand format. This helps your audience quickly grasp the key points and makes your content more shareable.

5. Visual storytelling: Use visuals to tell a story and evoke emotions. This can be done through videos, images with captions, or sequential imagery that guides the viewer through a narrative.

6. **User-generated content:** Incorporate user-generated content, such as customer photos or testimonials, into your visuals. This adds authenticity and credibility to your brand.

7. **Experiment with different formats:** Try different visual formats such as GIFs, animations, or interactive elements to make your visuals more engaging and memorable.

8. **Optimize for various platforms:** Ensure that your visuals are optimized for

different platforms and devices, including mobile devices. This includes resizing images and videos and adapting the layout to fit different screen sizes.

9. Use visual hierarchy: Arrange elements in your visuals to guide the viewer's attention. Use contrast, size, and placement to emphasize important elements and create a clear visual hierarchy.

10. Test and iterate: Continuously test different visuals and monitor their impact on your audience. Use analytics and feedback to iterate and improve your visuals over time.

Remember, attention-grabbing visuals can help you stand out in a crowded online marketplace and effectively communicate your brand's message. By investing time and effort in designing visually appealing content, you can enhance your online business's overall brand image and attract and retain customers.

Some examples of attention-grabbing visuals for online businesses include:

- **Eye-catching product images:** High-quality and visually appealing images of your products can entice customers to learn more or make a purchase.

- **Infographics:** Visual representations of data or information can be highly engaging and shareable, making them effective for conveying complex concepts or statistics.

- **Videos:** Dynamic and well-produced videos can capture viewers' attention and effectively demonstrate the use or benefits of your products or services.

- **Animated graphics:** GIFs or animations can add movement and interactivity to your visuals, making them more engaging and memorable.

- **User-generated content:** Sharing photos or videos submitted by your customers can not only provide social proof but also create a sense of community and authenticity around your brand.

- **Visual storytelling:** Using a series of visuals or images with captions to tell a narrative can captivate your audience and create an emotional connection.

Remember, the key is to create visuals that are visually appealing, aligned with your brand's identity, and relevant to your target audience. Experimenting with different formats and regularly analyzing the performance of your visuals can help you refine your approach and create visuals that effectively grab your audience's attention.

5.3 Utilizing Effective Copywriting Techniques

Effective copywriting involves creating compelling written content that persuades and encourages your audience to take action. It is an essential skill for online businesses to convert visitors into customers and drive sales.

Here are some key techniques to utilize when crafting copy for your online business:

1. **Understand your target audience:** Research and understand the demographics, needs, and desires of your target audience. Tailor your copy to resonate with their interests and motivations.

2. **Use persuasive language:** Write copy that incorporates persuasive words and phrases to influence your audience's decision-making. Highlight the benefits and solutions your products or services offer.

3. **Create compelling headlines:** Grab your audience's attention with attention-grabbing

headlines. A strong headline can entice readers to continue reading and engage with your content.

4. Focus on benefits, not just features: Clearly communicate the benefits your products or services provide. Explain how they can solve a problem or improve the customer's life rather than just listing features.

5. Incorporate social proof: Use testimonials, customer reviews, case studies, or social media mentions to provide evidence of the value and quality of your offerings. This helps to build trust and credibility with your audience.

6. Craft a clear and concise call-to-action (CTA): Guide your audience towards the desired action by including a clear and concise call-to-action. Use strong and action-oriented language to prompt them to make a purchase, sign up for a newsletter, or take any other desired action.

7. Use storytelling techniques: Connect with your audience on an emotional level through storytelling. Share personal anecdotes, customer success stories, or narratives that relate to your brand and products.

8. Incorporate SEO keywords: Optimize your copy for search engines by including relevant keywords that your target audience may use when searching for products or services like yours. This can help improve your search engine rankings and attract organic traffic to your website.

9. Use formatting and structure: Break up your copy into easily readable sections with subheadings, bullet points, and paragraphs. Use formatting techniques to highlight key points and create visual interest.

10. Edit and proofread: Before publishing your copy, thoroughly edit and proofread for grammar, spelling, and readability. Ensure that your content is error-free and easy to understand.

By utilizing these copywriting techniques, you can create persuasive and compelling content that engages your audience, builds trust, and drives conversions for your online business.

Chapter 6: Driving Traffic to Your Website

6.1 Search Engine Optimization (SEO) Strategies

Search Engine Optimization (SEO) strategies refer to the techniques and practices used to improve a website's visibility and ranking on search engine results pages (SERPs). The goal of SEO is to attract more organic (nonpaid) traffic to a website by optimizing various elements both on-page and off-page.

Some common SEO strategies include:

1. Keyword Research: Identifying relevant keywords and phrases that users are searching for and incorporating them into the website's content.

2. On-Page Optimization: Optimizing elements on individual webpages such as the page title, meta description, headings, URL structure, and content to make them more search-engine friendly.

3. Technical SEO: Ensuring that the website is technically optimized for search engines, including factors like website speed, mobile-friendliness, crawlability, and indexing.

4. Link Building: Building high-quality backlinks to the website from reputable and relevant sources to improve its authority and credibility.

5. Content Creation: Creating high-quality, original, and valuable content that targets specific keywords and provides valuable information to users.

6. User Experience Optimization: Improving the overall user experience of the website by optimizing its design, navigation, and site architecture.

7. Local SEO: Optimizing the website for local searches by including location-specific keywords, creating and optimizing Google My Business listings, and building local citations.

It's important to note that SEO is an ongoing process and requires continuous monitoring, analysis, and adjustments. It's also important to stay up to date with search engine algorithm updates and industry best practices to ensure your SEO efforts remain effective.

6.2 Social Media Marketing

Social media marketing involves utilizing various social media platforms to promote a business, engage with customers, and drive traffic to a website. It includes creating and sharing content, interacting with followers, and running paid advertising campaigns on platforms such as Facebook, Instagram, Twitter, LinkedIn, and YouTube.

Some strategies for effective social media marketing include:

1. **Social Media Strategy:** Developing a comprehensive strategy that aligns with business goals, target audience, and brand identity. This includes identifying the platforms to focus on, setting objectives, and determining key performance indicators (KPIs) to track success.

2. Content Creation: Creating valuable and engaging content specific to each platform and target audience. This can include a mix of text, images, videos, infographics, and other forms of media.

3. Community Engagement: Actively engaging with followers, responding to comments, messages, and reviews, and fostering a sense of community on social media. This helps build relationships, establish trust, and generate brand loyalty.

4. Influencer Marketing: Collaborating with influencers or industry experts who have a large and engaged following on social media. This can help expand reach, increase brand awareness, and drive traffic to your website.

5. Paid Advertising: Utilizing paid advertising options on social media platforms to reach a wider audience and target specific demographics. This can include running sponsored posts, creating targeted ads, and utilizing advanced targeting options to maximize the effectiveness of social media advertising.

6. Analytics and Measurement: Tracking and analyzing key metrics such as reach, engagement, conversions, and website traffic to evaluate the success of social media marketing campaigns. This data helps identify what is working and what can be improved upon.

It's important to have a consistent presence, provide valuable content, and engage with your audience on social media platforms. By effectively leveraging social media marketing, businesses can increase brand awareness, drive traffic to their website, generate leads, and ultimately boost sales.

6.3 Pay-Per-Click (PPC) Advertising

Pay-Per-Click (PPC) advertising is a digital marketing strategy where advertisers pay a fee for each click on their ads. It involves creating and running paid advertising campaigns on search engines like Google or Bing, as well as on social media platforms like Facebook, Instagram, or LinkedIn.

Some key aspects of PPC advertising include:

1.	**Keyword	Research:**
Identifying relevant keywords and phrases that potential customers are searching for and incorporating them into your PPC campaigns.

2.	**Ad Creation:** Developing compelling ad copy that captures attention and encourages users to click on your ads. This includes writing catchy headlines, clear descriptions, and utilizing relevant ad extensions.

3.	**Ad Targeting:** Utilizing targeting options to ensure your ads reach the right audience. This can include targeting based on geographic location, demographics, interests, and previous website interaction.

4. **Bid Management:** Setting bids for your keywords to determine how much you are willing to pay for each click. Effective bid management involves finding a balance between maximizing visibility and maintaining a profitable return on investment (ROI).

5. **Landing Page Optimization:** Creating dedicated landing pages that align with your PPC ads and provide a seamless user experience. Optimizing landing pages can improve conversion

rates and increase the likelihood of users taking desired actions, such as making a purchase or filling out a contact form.

6. Campaign Monitoring and Optimization: Regularly monitoring the performance of your PPC campaigns and making necessary adjustments. This can include tweaking keywords, ad copy, targeting options, and bid strategies to improve campaign efficiency and achieve desired goals.

7. Conversion Tracking: Implementing conversion tracking tools to measure the effectiveness of your PPC campaigns. This allows you to track the number of conversions generated, such as sales, sign-ups, or downloads, and calculate your return on ad spend (ROAS).

PPC advertising can be a highly effective way to drive targeted traffic to your website and increase online visibility. However, it requires careful planning, ongoing monitoring, and strategic optimization to ensure a positive ROI. It is important to regularly analyze and adjust your PPC campaigns based on performance data to maximize results and achieve your business goals.

Chapter 7: Building an Email List

7.1 Developing an Email Marketing Strategy

Developing an email marketing strategy is an essential part of any successful online business. It involves planning and implementing targeted campaigns to engage and nurture your email subscribers, ultimately driving them to take desired actions such as making a purchase or signing up for a service. Here are the key steps involved in developing an effective email marketing strategy:

1. **Set clear goals:** Determine what you want to achieve with your email marketing efforts. It could be increasing sales, driving website traffic, promoting new products or services, building customer loyalty, or generating leads. Having specific goals will guide your strategy and help measure its success.

2. Define your target audience: Segment your email subscribers based on their demographics, interests, purchase history, or any other relevant factors. This allows you to send more personalized and tailored messages that resonate with the interests and needs of each segment.

3. Build your email list: Continuously grow your email list by implementing lead generation tactics such as offering valuable content, discounts, or incentives in exchange for email sign-ups. Ensure compliance with data protection and privacy regulations when collecting and storing email addresses.

4. Create valuable content: Develop a content strategy that delivers value to your subscribers. This can include informative newsletters, exclusive offers, educational resources, customer success stories, or personalized recommendations. Make sure that your content is relevant, engaging, and provides a clear call to action.

5. Design visually appealing and mobile-friendly emails: Use eye-catching designs, compelling visuals, and responsive layouts that adapt to different devices. Incorporate your brand identity into your email templates to maintain consistency.

6. Automate your email campaigns: Implement automation tools to streamline your email marketing efforts. Set up automated welcome emails, abandoned cart reminders, and personalized follow-up sequences based on triggers such as user behavior or specific actions.

7. Test and optimize your campaigns: Continuously monitor the performance of your email campaigns by analyzing open rates, click-through rates, conversion rates, and other relevant metrics. Conduct A/B testing to experiment with different subject lines, email copy, call to actions, or visuals to identify what resonates best with your audience.

8. Maintain email deliverability: Ensure your emails reach your subscribers' inboxes by following email deliverability best practices. This includes using reputable email service providers, optimizing your sender reputation, regularly cleaning your email list, and avoiding spammy tactics.

9. Personalize and segment your emails: Leverage the data you have on your subscribers to personalize your email content and offers. Use segmentation techniques to send targeted messages to specific groups within your audience, increasing the relevancy and effectiveness of your campaigns.

10. Monitor and analyze results: Track the performance of your email marketing campaigns using analytics tools. Pay attention to key metrics like open rates, click-through rates, conversion rates, and unsubscribe rates. Use this data to refine your strategy and make data-driven decisions.

11. Maintain compliance with regulations: Ensure that your email marketing practices comply with applicable laws and regulations such as the General Data Protection Regulation (GDPR) or the CAN-SPAM Act. Obtain proper consent from subscribers, provide clear unsubscribe options, and handle personal data securely.

12. Continuously optimize and iterate: Regularly review and optimize your email marketing strategy based on the insights gained from data analysis and customer feedback. Experiment with different tactics, explore new technologies, and stay updated with industry trends to keep your campaigns fresh and effective.

By developing a well-thought-out email marketing strategy, you can build strong relationships with your subscribers, drive conversions, and grow your online business effectively.

7.2 Creating Lead Magnet Offers

Creating lead magnet offers is an essential step in building an email list for your online business. Lead magnets are valuable free resources or incentives that you offer to your website visitors in exchange for their email addresses. These offers help to attract and capture the attention of your target audience, encouraging them to provide their contact information and become potential leads for your business.

To create effective lead magnet offers, consider the following steps:

1. Identify your target audience: Before creating a lead magnet, it's crucial to understand the needs, pain points, and interests of your target audience. This will help you tailor your offer to provide maximum value and relevance.

2. Choose a valuable resource: Your lead magnet should offer something of value to your audience. It could be an ebook, a checklist, a guide, a template, a video tutorial, a free course, or any other valuable content that addresses a specific problem or provides a solution to a particular need.

3. Solve a problem or address a pain point: A lead magnet should directly address a problem or pain point that your target audience is facing. Consider the common challenges or questions they might have and create a resource that provides a solution or valuable information related to those issues.

4. Create compelling content: Make sure the content of your lead magnet is well-written, well-designed, and engaging. Use clear and concise language, include visuals and examples if applicable, and make it easy for your audience to understand and apply the information you provide.

5. Make it easily accessible: Ensure that your lead magnet is easily downloadable or accessible by providing a clear and prominent call-to-action

(CTA) on your website or landing page. Use a form or opt-in box to collect email addresses in exchange for the lead magnet.

6. Promote your lead magnet: Once your lead magnet is created and accessible, promote it through various channels such as your website, blog posts, social media platforms, email newsletters, and online advertisements. Make sure to highlight the value and benefits of your lead magnet to attract potential leads.

7. Follow up with email campaigns: Once you have

collected email addresses through your lead magnet, it's important to have a follow-up plan in place. Utilize email marketing campaigns to nurture and engage your leads further, providing them with additional valuable content, special offers, or exclusive access to your products or services.

Remember that your lead magnet should align with your overall business goals and target audience. Continuously analyze and evaluate the performance of your lead magnet offers to optimize and improve their effectiveness in attracting and converting leads for your online business

7.3 Crafting Compelling Email Campaigns

Crafting compelling email campaigns is an essential aspect of successful online business marketing. It involves creating engaging and persuasive emails that resonate with your audience and encourage them to take desired actions, such as making a purchase, subscribing to a service, or sharing your content. Here are some key elements and strategies to consider when crafting compelling email campaigns:

1. Segment your audience: Divide your email list into various segments based on factors such as demographics, purchase history, or engagement levels. This allows you to tailor your messages to specific groups, increasing the relevance and effectiveness of your campaigns.

2. Personalize your emails: Use the recipient's name and personalize the content based on their preferences, interests, or past interactions. This adds a personalized touch and makes the email feel more relevant and meaningful.

3. Create attention-grabbing subject lines: Your subject line is the first thing recipients see, so it needs to be compelling enough to entice them to open the email. Use strong and concise language, convey urgency or exclusivity, or ask intriguing questions to generate interest.

4. Provide valuable and relevant content: The content of your email should offer something of value to the recipient, whether it's informative articles, exclusive discounts, or personalized recommendations. Make sure the content aligns with their interests and needs, and addresses their pain points or desires.

5. Use persuasive and engaging copy: Write clear and concise copy that grabs attention, maintains interest, and compels recipients to take action. Use persuasive language, emphasize the benefits, and include a strong call to action (CTA) that prompts them to click, purchase, or engage further.

6. Incorporate eye-catching visuals: Images and graphics can enhance the visual appeal of your emails and make them more engaging. Use high-quality visuals that relate to your message and product/service, and ensure they load quickly and are compatible with various devices.

7. Optimize for mobile: With the increasing use of smartphones, it's crucial to ensure your emails are mobile-friendly. Use responsive design that adapts to different screen sizes, keep your content concise and scannable, and use larger fonts and buttons for easy navigation and interaction.

8. A/B testing: Experiment with different elements such as subject lines, CTA placement, email layouts, or visuals to see which variations generate better results. Perform A/B tests by sending different versions of your email to a smaller portion of your audience and analyzing the performance metrics to determine the most effective approach.

9. Monitor and analyze performance: Track metrics such

as open rates, click-through rates, conversion rates, and unsubscribe rates to evaluate the success of your email campaigns. Use email marketing analytics tools to gain insights into what is working and what needs improvement. Regularly review and analyze these metrics to make data-driven decisions and optimize future campaigns.

10. Test and iterate: Email marketing is an ongoing process of continuous improvement. Based on the insights gained from analyzing data, make necessary adjustments to your campaigns, content, and strategies. Test different approaches, monitor results, and iterate to refine and optimize your email marketing efforts.

By implementing these strategies and continuously refining your approach, you can create compelling email campaigns that effectively engage and convert your audience, leading to increased sales, customer loyalty, and business growth.

Chapter 8: Providing Excellent Customer Service

8.1   Establishing   Customer Support Channels

Establishing customer support channels refers to creating various methods for customers to reach out to your business and receive assistance or resolve any issues they may have. This is an important aspect of providing excellent customer service and ensuring customer satisfaction.

Customer support channels can include:

1. Phone support: Setting up a dedicated phone line for customers to call and speak with a representative. This allows for direct and immediate communication with customers.

2. Email support: Providing an email address or contact form for customers to send their inquiries or issues to. This allows for asynchronous communication and gives customers the opportunity to provide detailed information.

3. Live chat support: Implementing a live chat feature on your website where customers can chat with a representative in real-time. This provides instant assistance and can help resolve issues quickly.

4. Social media support: Monitoring and responding to customer inquiries or complaints on social media platforms. Many customers prefer using social media to voice their concerns, so it's important to have a dedicated support team managing these channels.

5. Self-service support: Creating a knowledge base or FAQ section on your website where customers can find answers to common questions or problems. This allows customers to troubleshoot and find solutions on their own.

6. Community forums or online discussion boards: Providing a platform where customers can interact with each other, ask questions, and share their experiences. This can create a sense of community and allow customers to help each other.

When establishing customer support channels, it's important to consider the needs and preferences of your target audience. Some customers may prefer phone support for immediate assistance, while others may prefer email or chat for convenience. It's essential to offer multiple channels to accommodate different customer preferences.

In addition, it's crucial to have a well-trained and knowledgeable support team to handle customer inquiries and issues effectively. Customer support representatives should be trained in product knowledge, problem-solving, and empathy to provide a positive experience for customers.

By establishing various customer support channels and providing excellent service, you can build trust and loyalty with your customers and differentiate your business from competitors. This can ultimately lead to customer retention and positive word-of-mouth referrals, which are crucial for the success of your online business.

8.2 Responding to Customer Inquiries and Issues

In this chapter, we will discuss the importance of responding to customer inquiries and issues promptly and effectively. This is a crucial aspect of providing excellent customer service and keeping your customers satisfied.

When customers have questions, concerns, or encounter problems with your products or services, it is essential to address their issues in a timely manner. Here are some key points to consider when responding to customer inquiries and issues:

1. Promptness: Make sure to respond to customer inquiries and issues as quickly as possible. This shows that you value their time and are committed to resolving their concerns.

2. Active listening: When interacting with customers, make sure to actively listen to their concerns and fully understand their issues. Take the time to ask clarifying questions if needed and show empathy towards their situation.

3. Personalization: Treat each customer as an individual and personalize your responses. Address them by name and use their specific concerns or issues in your response. This helps to create a more personalized and positive customer experience.

4. Clear communication: Use clear and concise language when communicating with customers. Avoid technical jargon or complex explanations that may confuse them further. Instead, provide simple and straightforward solutions or answers to their inquiries.

5. Offer solutions: When addressing customer issues, provide practical solutions or alternatives that can resolve their problems. If necessary, involve relevant departments or team members to ensure the best resolution for the customer.

6. Follow-up: After resolving a customer's issue, make sure to follow up with them to ensure their satisfaction. This can be through a phone call, email, or survey. This demonstrates your commitment to their experience and shows that you value their feedback.

7. Escalation process: In some cases, customer inquiries or issues may require escalation to higher-level support or management. Have clear protocols in place for when this is necessary. Ensure that your customer service team is trained to identify situations that require escalation and knows how to handle them.

8. Document customer interactions: Keep a record of all customer inquiries, issues, and resolutions. This helps in keeping track of recurring problems, identifying patterns, and improving your customer service processes over time.

Remember, providing excellent customer service goes a long way in building customer loyalty and creating positive word-of-mouth for your business. By responding promptly and effectively to customer inquiries and issues, you can enhance customer satisfaction and ultimately contribute to the success of your online business.

In conclusion, responding to customer inquiries and issues is an important aspect of providing excellent customer service. It involves promptness, active listening, personalization, clear communication, offering solutions, follow-up, having an escalation process, and documenting customer interactions. By effectively addressing customer concerns and resolving their issues, you can ensure customer satisfaction and build long-term relationships.

8.3 Turning Dissatisfied Customers into Loyal Advocates

While it's inevitable that you may encounter unsatisfied

customers at some point, it's crucial to address their concerns and successfully resolve their issues to win them back and transform their negative experience into a positive one.

Here are some strategies to effectively turn dissatisfied customers into loyal advocates:

1. **Active listening:** When dealing with a dissatisfied customer, it's important to actively listen to their grievances and frustrations. Allow them to express their concerns without interruption and show empathy towards their situation. Understand their

perspective and make them feel heard.

2. Apologize and take responsibility: Take responsibility for any mistakes or shortcomings that may have contributed to the customer's dissatisfaction. Offer a sincere apology and acknowledge any inconveniences caused. This demonstrates accountability and shows the customer that their concerns are taken seriously.

3. Find a solution: Work with the customer to find a suitable resolution to their issue. Understand their desired outcome and collaborate with them to find a mutually beneficial solution. Offer alternatives or extras as a way of compensating for their negative experience.

4. Go above and beyond: Exceed the customer's expectations by going the extra mile to resolve their problem. This may involve providing additional assistance, offering discounts or refunds, or providing personalized solutions. By demonstrating your commitment to their satisfaction, you can turn their negative experience into a positive one.

5. **Regular communication:** Keep the customer updated throughout the resolution process. Communicate the steps you are taking to address their concerns and provide a timeline for resolution. Regularly check in with them to ensure their satisfaction and address any additional questions or issues that arise.

6. **Follow-up and feedback:** Once the issue is resolved, follow up with the customer to ensure their satisfaction. Ask for feedback on their overall experience and use their input to improve your processes. This shows that you value their

opinion and are committed to continuous improvement.

7. Provide incentives: Offer incentives to customers who had a negative experience with your business. This can include discounts on future purchases, exclusive offers, or access to premium content. By providing these incentives, you can encourage them to give your business another chance and become loyal advocates.

8. Empower your customer service team: Ensure that your customer service team has the necessary resources, training, and authority to effectively handle customer complaints and resolve issues. Empower them to make decisions and provide solutions independently, without needing constant supervision or approval. This enables them to address dissatisfied customers promptly and efficiently, increasing the chances of turning them into loyal advocates.

9. Learn from the experience: Take the opportunity to learn from the mistakes that led to the customer's dissatisfaction. Identify areas for improvement in your products, services, or processes, and implement necessary changes to prevent similar issues in the future. Use the feedback received to continuously enhance the customer experience.

10. Maintain ongoing relationships: After successfully resolving the customer's issue, continue to nurture the relationship. Keep in touch with personalized emails, exclusive offers, or VIP programs. By staying engaged with the customer, you can build long-term loyalty and turn them into advocates who promote your online business to others.

Remember, every dissatisfied customer has the potential to become a loyal advocate if their concerns are addressed effectively. By actively listening, apologizing, finding solutions, going above and beyond, maintaining regular communication, providing incentives, empowering your customer service team, learning from the experience, and nurturing relationships, you can turn dissatisfied customers into valuable advocates for your online business.

In conclusion, turning dissatisfied customers into loyal advocates is a critical aspect of providing excellent customer service. By actively addressing their concerns, finding solutions, going above and beyond, maintaining regular communication, providing incentives, empowering your customer service team, learning from the experience, and nurturing ongoing relationships, you can transform their negative experience into a positive one. This not only retains the customer but also creates loyal advocates who can promote your business to others and contribute to its success.

Chapter 9: Analyzing Data and Making Data-Driven Decisions

Analyzing data and making data-driven decisions is an essential aspect of running an online business. It involves collecting and analyzing relevant data to gain insights into various aspects of the business, such as customer behavior, sales performance, website traffic, and marketing effectiveness. This data is then used to inform decision-making and drive strategic actions.

9.1 Understanding Key Metrics for Online Businesses

Understanding key metrics for online businesses is crucial for monitoring and evaluating the performance of your online business. These metrics provide valuable insights into various aspects of your business, such as customer behavior, website performance, marketing effectiveness, and overall profitability. By understanding and analyzing these metrics, you can make data-driven decisions to optimize your business strategies and drive growth.

Some of the key metrics for online businesses include:

1. **Conversion Rate:** This metric measures the percentage of website visitors who complete a desired action, such as making a purchase, filling out a lead form, or subscribing to a newsletter. A

high conversion rate indicates that your website and marketing efforts are effectively driving desired user actions.

2. Customer Acquisition Cost (CAC): CAC refers to the amount of money you spend to acquire a new customer. This metric includes marketing and advertising expenses, sales commissions, and any other costs associated with acquiring a new customer. It is important to keep your CAC in check to ensure that the cost of acquiring customers does not exceed their lifetime value.

3. Average Order Value (AOV): AOV is the average amount a customer spends per transaction on your website. Increasing your AOV can contribute to higher revenue and profitability. This can be achieved by implementing upsell and cross-sell strategies or offering bundle deals and promotions.

4. Customer Lifetime Value (CLV): CLV measures the total revenue generated by a customer throughout their relationship with your business. This metric helps you understand the long-term value of each customer and allows you to allocate resources and prioritize retention strategies accordingly.

5. Return on Investment (ROI): ROI measures the profitability of your marketing and advertising campaigns. It calculates the ratio of the net profit generated from a campaign to the total cost of that campaign. By analyzing ROI, you can determine which marketing channels and strategies are most effective and allocate your budget appropriately.

6. Website Traffic and User Engagement: Monitoring website traffic metrics, such as the number of visitors, pageviews, and bounce rate, can help you understand the overall performance and user experience of your website. Analyzing user engagement metrics, such as time spent on site, click-through rates, and conversion paths, can provide valuable insights into the effectiveness of your content and website design.

7. Customer Satisfaction and Net Promoter Score (NPS): Measuring customer satisfaction and NPS helps assess the loyalty and advocacy of your customers. By collecting feedback and monitoring NPS, you can identify areas for improvement and address any issues or concerns to foster a positive customer experience.

Understanding these key metrics and regularly analyzing them can help you identify strengths and weaknesses in your online business, make data-driven decisions, and optimize your strategies to drive growth and profitability. It is important to monitor these metrics regularly and track them over time to identify trends and patterns that can guide your business decisions.

9.2 Setting Up Tracking and Analytics Tools

Setting up tracking and analytics tools is essential for accurately measuring and analyzing the key metrics mentioned earlier. These tools provide valuable insights into user behavior, website performance, marketing effectiveness, and overall business metrics. Here are some important steps to consider when setting up tracking and analytics tools for your online business:

1. Choose the Right Analytics Platform: There are several popular analytics platforms available, such as Google Analytics, Adobe Analytics, and Mixpanel. Evaluate your needs and choose the platform that best aligns with your business goals and budget.

2. Install Tracking Codes: Once you have chosen an analytics platform, you will need to install its tracking code on your website. This code collects data about website visitors and their interactions, which is then sent to the analytics platform for analysis.

3. Set Up Goals and Conversion Tracking: Define your business goals and set up conversion tracking within your analytics platform. This will allow you to track specific actions that are important to your business, such as purchases, form submissions, or email sign-ups.

4. Implement Event Tracking: Event tracking allows you to track specific user interactions on your website, such as clicks on buttons, downloads of files, or video views. Implement event tracking to gain insights into user engagement and behavior.

5. Analyze Data and Generate Reports: Once your tracking and analytics tools are set up and collecting data, it's important to regularly analyze that data and generate reports. Look for trends, patterns, and areas of improvement in your website performance, marketing campaigns, and overall business metrics. Use these insights to make data-driven decisions and optimize your online business.

6. Customize Dashboards: Most analytics platforms allow you to customize dashboards, which provide a snapshot of your key metrics and data visualizations. Customize your dashboard to display the metrics that are most relevant to your business goals and regularly monitor them.

7. Conduct A/B Testing: A/B testing is a method of comparing two versions of a webpage or marketing campaign to determine which one performs better. Use A/B testing to test different website layouts, landing pages, marketing messages, and calls-to-action. This will help you optimize your website and marketing campaigns for better results.

8. Seek Help from Data Analysts or Consultants: If you are not familiar or comfortable with data analysis and interpretation, consider seeking help from data analysts or consultants. They can provide valuable insights and recommendations based on your data, helping you make informed decisions for your online business.

By setting up tracking and analytics tools, you can gain valuable insights into your online business's performance, user behavior, and marketing efforts. This information will help you make informed decisions, identify areas of improvement, and optimize your strategies for better results.

9.3 Using Data to Optimize and Scale Your Business

Once you have implemented tracking and analytics tools and collected data about your online business, it's important to utilize that data to optimize and scale your operations. Here are some ways to leverage data for growth:

1. **Identify Key Performance Indicators (KPIs):** Determine the

most important metrics for your business's success. These may include conversion rate, customer acquisition cost, average order value, or customer retention rate. By focusing on these KPIs, you can prioritize areas of improvement and drive positive results.

2. Conduct A/B Testing: Use data to test and compare different strategies and approaches. A/B testing allows you to compare two versions of a webpage, marketing campaign, or pricing structure to see which performs better. Make data-driven decisions by implementing changes based on the results of A/B tests to optimize conversion rates and customer engagement.

3. Personalize User Experiences: Analyze data on user behavior and preferences to personalize the customer experience. Use information such as past purchases, browsing history, and demographics to provide tailored recommendations, personalized emails, and targeted marketing campaigns. This customization can enhance customer satisfaction and increase engagement.

4. Implement Retargeting Campaigns: Use data on user behavior to create retargeting campaigns. If a user visits your website and leaves without making a purchase, you can use retargeting to show them relevant ads as they browse other websites or social media platforms. This can help bring them back to your site and encourage them to complete their purchase.

5. Optimize Marketing Channels: Use data to determine the most effective marketing channels for driving traffic and conversions.

Analyze the performance of different channels such as search engines, social media platforms, email campaigns, and affiliate programs. Allocate your marketing budget and resources accordingly to maximize ROI and reach your target audience.

6. Monitor Customer Feedback: Utilize tools such as online reviews, surveys, and customer feedback forms to gather insights from your customers. Analyze this data to identify areas for improvement and address any customer concerns or issues. By proactively addressing feedback, you can enhance customer satisfaction and build loyalty.

7. Forecast and Budget: Use historical data and analytics to forecast future trends and plan your budget accordingly. By understanding patterns in sales, traffic, and customer behavior, you can make informed decisions about inventory management, marketing spend, and resource allocation.

8. Stay Agile and Iterate: Continuously analyze and adapt to changing data trends and customer behaviors. Use the insights gained from your data to make iterative improvements to your online business. Stay up-to-date with industry trends and innovations to ensure your business remains competitive in the online marketplace.

By using data to optimize and scale your online business, you can make informed decisions, drive growth, and improve the overall success and profitability of your venture.

Chapter 10: Scaling Your Online Business

10.1　Outsourcing and Delegating Tasks

As your online business grows, it may become challenging to handle every task on your own. Outsourcing and delegating specific tasks can help you streamline operations, improve efficiency, and focus on core areas of your business.

Here are some key considerations when it comes to outsourcing and delegating:

1. **Identify Your Strengths and Weaknesses:** Assess your own skills and expertise to determine which tasks you excel at and which ones you struggle with. Identify areas where you may lack the necessary knowledge or experience. This will help you prioritize tasks that can be outsourced or delegated.

2. **Determine Core Business Functions:** Identify the core functions of your business that

require your direct attention and cannot be easily outsourced. These may include strategic planning, product development, customer relationship management, or business development. Focus on these core functions and consider outsourcing or delegating other tasks.

3. Make a List of Outsourcing Opportunities: Make a list of tasks that can be outsourced or delegated. This may include graphic design, content writing, social media management, customer support, or accounting/bookkeeping. Determine what skills or expertise are required for each task.

4. Find Reliable Service Providers: Research and identify reliable service providers who can handle the tasks you want to outsource. Look for providers who have experience and expertise in your industry, and check their references and reviews. Consider using freelancing platforms or hiring virtual assistants.

5. Clearly Define Tasks and Expectations: Clearly communicate your expectations, deadlines, and desired outcomes to the service providers or individuals you delegate tasks to. Provide detailed instructions and guidelines to ensure that the work is done according to your requirements.

6. Set Up Communication and Collaboration Systems: Establish effective communication and collaboration systems with your service providers or team members. Utilize project management tools, file sharing platforms, and communication channels (such as email or video conferencing) to stay connected and track progress.

7. Monitor and Evaluate Performance: Regularly monitor

the performance of your outsourced tasks or delegated responsibilities. Provide feedback and guidance to ensure that the work meets your standards. Make adjustments or seek alternative providers if necessary.

8. Consider Cost vs. Value: Evaluate the cost vs. value proposition of outsourcing or delegating tasks. Determine whether the benefits gained from outsourcing outweigh the costs involved. Calculate the potential savings in time, effort, and resources.

Remember that outsourcing or delegating tasks may not always be the best approach for every business or situation. Assess the pros and cons, and make informed decisions based on your specific needs and circumstances. As your business evolves, regularly reevaluate your outsourcing and delegation strategies to ensure efficiency and effectiveness.

10.2 Expanding Your Product Line or Service offerings

Expanding your product line or service offerings is an essential strategy for growth and increased revenue in your online business. Here are some key considerations when it comes to expanding your offerings:

1. Understand Your Target Market: Start by understanding your target market and their needs. Conduct market research to identify potential gaps or opportunities in the market that align with your business and customer base.

2. Identify Complementary Products or Services: Look for products or services that are complementary to your existing offerings. Consider what products or services would naturally fit with your current brand and customer base. For example, if you sell beauty products, you could consider expanding into skincare or haircare products.

3. Conduct Competitive Analysis: Research your competitors to see what products or services they offer. Identify areas where you can differentiate yourself or fill gaps that your competitors may have overlooked. This will help you determine the most viable expansion opportunities.

4. Test and Validate: Before fully committing to expanding your offerings, consider testing the market with a smaller-scale launch or pilot program. This can help you gauge customer interest and demand, gather feedback, and make any necessary adjustments before a full launch.

5. Ensure Quality and Consistency: Maintain the same level of quality and consistency with your new offerings as you do with your existing products or services. This will help to maintain customer trust and loyalty.

6. Update Your Website and Marketing Materials: Once you have expanded your offerings, update your website and marketing materials to reflect the new products or services. Ensure that your messaging is clear and cohesive across all channels.

7. Train Your Team: If you have a team, make sure they are trained and knowledgeable about the new offerings. They should be able to answer any questions customers may have and provide support and assistance.

8. Monitor and Evaluate: Continuously monitor the performance of your new offerings. Track sales, customer feedback, and any other relevant metrics to assess the success of the expansion. Use this data to make informed decisions and adjustments as needed.

By expanding your product line or service offerings, you can attract new customers, increase customer loyalty, and ultimately grow your online business.

10.3 Partnering or Collaborating with Other Businesses

Partnering or collaborating with other businesses can be a strategic move to expand your online business and reach a wider audience. Here are some key considerations when it comes to forming partnerships or collaborations:

1. **Identify Compatible Businesses:** Look for businesses that align with your brand and target market. Consider businesses that offer

complementary products or services or businesses that have a similar target audience. For example, if you sell fitness apparel, you could partner with a fitness equipment company or a fitness influencer.

2. Define Shared Goals and Objectives: Before entering into a partnership or collaboration, it's important to define shared goals and objectives. Determine how the collaboration will benefit both parties and what each party hopes to achieve. This will help ensure a mutually beneficial partnership.

3. Establish Clear Roles and Responsibilities: Clearly define the roles and responsibilities of each party involved in the partnership or collaboration. This will help avoid confusion or conflicts down the line. Determine who will handle what aspects of the collaboration and establish effective communication channels.

4. Outline Terms and Agreements: Create a formal agreement or contract that outlines the terms and conditions of the partnership or collaboration. Include details such as duration, financial arrangements, intellectual property rights, and any other relevant terms. Consult with a legal professional if necessary to ensure that the agreement protects the interests of both parties.

5. Foster Open Communication: Effective communication is key to a successful partnership or collaboration. Maintain regular communication with your partners to ensure a smooth workflow and to address any issues or concerns that may arise. Be transparent and open to feedback and suggestions from your partners.

6. Leverage Each Other's Networks: One of the main advantages of partnering or collaborating with other businesses is the opportunity to tap into their existing customer base or network. Take advantage of this by cross-promoting each other's products or services, hosting joint marketing campaigns, or creating special offers or discounts for customers of both businesses.

7. Measure and Evaluate Results: Regularly monitor and evaluate the results of your partnership or collaboration. Track key performance indicators (KPIs) such as increased website traffic, sales conversions, or customer engagement. This will help you assess the effectiveness of the collaboration and make any necessary adjustments or improvements.

Remember, partnerships and collaborations can be beneficial for both parties involved, but it's important to choose your partners wisely and establish clear expectations and agreements. By working together, you can leverage each other's strengths and resources to drive growth for your online business.

Chapter 11: Legal and Financial Considerations

11.1 Registering Your Business and Obtaining Licenses

Registering your business and obtaining licenses are crucial steps for any online entrepreneur to legally operate their business. Here is an explanation of these processes:

1. Registering Your Business:

- Registering your business involves officially establishing it as a legal entity with the appropriate government agencies or authorities. The specific registration requirements can vary depending on the country and jurisdiction in which you operate.

- The primary purpose of registering your business is to give it legal recognition and separate it from your personal assets. This protects you from personal liability in case of any legal disputes or financial issues.

- Registering your business typically involves choosing a

business name, filing the necessary documents, and paying the required registration fees. This process may involve registering with the local government, state or provincial authorities, and possibly the national government as well.

- Registering your business also ensures that your business name is unique and legally protected, preventing others from using the same name or causing confusion in the marketplace.

2. Obtaining Licenses:

- Depending on the nature of your online business and the industry you operate in, you may need to obtain certain licenses or permits to comply with legal regulations and operate legally.

- Licenses and permits can vary widely based on factors such as your location, the products or services you offer, and any specialized regulations that apply to your industry (e.g., health, food, finance, etc.).

- Common licenses and permits for online businesses may include general business licenses, sales tax permits, professional licenses (for certain industries), and any industry-specific permits or certifications.

- To obtain licenses, you will typically need to research the specific requirements for your industry and location, complete the necessary application forms, and meet any eligibility criteria (such as educational or experience requirements). Additionally, you may need to pay application fees or undergo inspections to ensure compliance with safety or health standards.

- It is important to note that the requirements for licenses and permits may vary depending on your jurisdiction and the specific regulations that apply to your industry. Therefore, it is crucial to consult with local authorities or seek legal advice to ensure that you are in compliance with all necessary licensing requirements.

By registering your business and obtaining the appropriate licenses, you establish a legal foundation for your online business, ensuring compliance with government regulations and protecting yourself and your business from potential legal issues.

11.2 Understanding Tax Obligations for Online Businesses

Running an online business also means understanding your tax obligations and ensuring compliance with tax laws. Here are some important considerations:

- **Determine your tax jurisdiction:** Your tax obligations will depend on your business's location and the jurisdictions in which you have customers or operate. Each jurisdiction may have different tax laws and requirements.

- **Register for tax purposes:** You may need to register your business with the appropriate tax authorities, such as obtaining a Tax Identification Number (TIN) or an Employer Identification Number (EIN).

- **Sales tax:** If your business sells physical products, you may be required to collect and remit sales tax to the relevant states or countries where your customers are located. Research the sales tax laws in each jurisdiction to understand your obligations.

- **Value-added tax (VAT):** Depending on your location and the countries you do business with, you may need to handle VAT obligations. VAT is a consumption tax that is typically collected on goods and services in certain countries.

- **Income tax:** As an online business owner, you will likely need to report and pay income tax on the profits earned by your business. Consult with a tax professional to understand the specific income tax obligations for your business and ensure accurate reporting.

- **Deductions and exemptions:** It's important to keep track of your business expenses and understand what deductions and exemptions you may be eligible for. This can help lower your taxable income and reduce your overall tax liability. Common deductions for online businesses may include expenses related to website hosting, marketing and advertising, office supplies, shipping and fulfillment costs, and professional services.

- **Hiring employees or independent contractors:** If you hire employees or work with independent contractors, you'll need to understand your obligations regarding payroll taxes, such as withholding and remitting income tax, Social Security, and Medicare taxes. It's important to comply with employment tax laws and regulations to avoid penalties.

- **International tax considerations:** If you conduct business internationally, you'll need to understand any tax treaties or agreements between your home country and the countries you do business with. Cross-border transactions may have specific tax implications, such as withholding taxes on payments to foreign vendors or tax reporting requirements for foreign income.

To ensure compliance with tax regulations, it's advisable to work with a qualified tax professional who specializes in online businesses. They can help you navigate the complexities of tax regulations, identify tax-saving opportunities, and ensure accurate reporting and filing of your business taxes.

11.3 Protecting Your Intellectual Property

As an online business owner, it's crucial to protect your intellectual property, which includes your brand, logo, website content, products, and any original creations you produce. Here are some key considerations:

-    **Trademarks:**   Consider registering trademarks for your brand name, logo, and any distinctive marks that identify your business. Trademarks provide legal protection and exclusive rights to use your brand in connection with your goods or services. Conduct a thorough search to ensure your chosen trademarks are available and not infringing on existing trademarks.

- **Copyrights:** Copyright laws automatically protect original works of authorship, such as website content, images, videos, and software code. It's advisable to prominently display a copyright notice (e.g., © Year, Your Company Name) on your website. If you have unique content or creations, consider registering copyrights to enhance legal protection.

- **Patents:** If you have invented a unique product or technology, you may consider seeking a patent to protect your invention from being copied or used without your permission. Patents provide exclusive rights to the inventor for a limited period, allowing you to commercialize and control the use of the invention.

- **Trade secrets:** Certain aspects of your business, such as proprietary processes, formulas, customer lists or business strategies, may qualify as trade secrets. Protect trade secrets through confidentiality agreements with employees, contractors, and partners, and implement security measures to prevent unauthorized access or disclosure.

- **Domain name protection:** Register your domain name and

variations of it to prevent others from using similar domains that could confuse customers or dilute your brand's value. Consider using domain privacy services to keep your personal information private.

- **Terms of Use and Privacy Policy**: Clearly outline the terms and conditions for using your website and the privacy practices you follow. This helps protect your business from liability and ensures compliance with privacy laws.

- **Contracts and agreements**: Use written contracts and

agreements when working with vendors, suppliers, contractors, or employees. These should specify the terms of the relationship, ownership of intellectual property, confidentiality obligations, and any limitations or permissions regarding the use of your intellectual property.

- **Enforcing your rights:** If you discover someone infringing on your intellectual property, consult with an intellectual property attorney to understand your options for enforcement, such as sending cease and desist letters or filing lawsuits.

It's important to consult with legal professionals specializing in intellectual property laws to ensure you fully understand and protect your rights.

Chapter 12: Never Stop Learning and Innovating

12.1 Staying Up to Date with Industry Trends and Technologies

In the ever-evolving world of online businesses, it's crucial to stay updated with the latest industry trends and technologies. This allows you to remain competitive, adapt to changing customer preferences, and take advantage of new opportunities. Here's why staying up to date is important and how you can do it effectively:

Importance of staying up to date:

1. Competitive advantage: By keeping up with industry trends, you can identify new strategies, techniques, and technologies that give you a competitive edge over your rivals. This can help you differentiate your business and attract more customers.

2. Customer satisfaction: Understanding the latest trends and technologies helps you meet and exceed customer expectations. By delivering cutting-edge solutions and experiences, you can enhance customer satisfaction and loyalty.

3. **Market insights:** Staying informed about industry trends allows you to gain valuable insights into market dynamics, consumer behavior, and emerging opportunities. This knowledge can guide your decision-making and help you identify untapped markets or niches.

4. **Innovation and growth:** Being aware of technological advancements and industry best practices empowers you to innovate and develop new products, services, or business models. This can support business growth and help you stay ahead of competitors.

Methods for staying up to date:

1. Industry publications and news: Subscribe to relevant industry publications, newsletters, and blogs. These sources often provide insights into emerging trends, case studies, and expert opinions. Stay updated on the latest news and developments in your industry.

2. Networking and events: Attend industry conferences, seminars, webinars, and trade shows. These events provide opportunities to connect with industry experts, learn from thought leaders, and gain insights into emerging technologies and trends. Network with peers in your field to share knowledge and experiences.

3. Online communities and forums: Join online communities, forums, and social media groups related to your industry. Engage in discussions, ask questions, and learn from the collective wisdom of community members. Platforms like LinkedIn, Reddit, and industry-specific forums can be excellent sources of information.

4. Continuous education and courses: Enroll in online courses, webinars, or workshops to learn about new technologies, marketing strategies, or industry-specific skills. Many educational platforms offer courses specifically tailored to online business owners.

5. Industry influencers and thought leaders: Follow industry influencers and thought leaders on social media platforms. They often share valuable insights, trends, and expertise. Engage with their content, leave comments, and participate in discussions to deepen your knowledge.

6. **Research and analysis:** Conduct regular research and analysis of your industry, competitors, and target market. Monitor market reports, consumer surveys, and competitor analysis to identify trends and patterns. Utilize tools like Google Trends, industry reports, and market research firms to gather data and insights.

7. **Stay updated on technology advancements:** Keep an eye on

technological advancements that can potentially impact your industry. This includes emerging technologies like artificial intelligence, virtual reality, blockchain, or any other innovations relevant to your business. Stay informed about their potential applications and how they can be leveraged to enhance your products, services, or operations.

Remember, staying up to date is an ongoing process, and it's important to allocate dedicated time and resources for learning and staying informed. By actively seeking knowledge, staying curious, and embracing change, you can position your online business for long-term success in a dynamic and ever-changing marketplace.

12.2 Continuing Education and Professional Development

Continuing education and professional development are essential for online entrepreneurs to stay relevant and succeed in their industry. Here are some key reasons to prioritize ongoing learning and how you can embrace professional development:

Benefits of continuing education and professional development:

1. Enhance skills and expertise: The online business landscape is constantly evolving, and new skills and knowledge are required to stay competitive. By engaging in continuous education, you can enhance your existing skills, learn new techniques, and stay updated with industry best practices.

2. Adapt to industry changes: Industries undergo rapid changes due to advancements in technology, shifts in consumer behavior, and evolving market trends. Continuous education helps you adapt to these changes, ensuring your business remains agile and responsive to market needs.

3. Expand your network: Professional development opportunities, such as conferences, workshops, and courses, provide networking opportunities. Connecting with industry peers, experts, and mentors can lead to valuable collaborations, partnerships, and knowledge sharing.

4. Boost confidence and credibility: Staying up to date

with the latest knowledge and skills boosts your confidence in your abilities as an online entrepreneur. It also enhances your credibility among clients, customers, and industry peers, positioning you as an expert in your field.

5. Personal and professional growth: Continuing education and professional development promote personal and professional growth. It encourages self-improvement, broadens your perspectives, and fosters a mindset of lifelong learning. It can also lead to new opportunities, career advancements, and increased job satisfaction.

Ways to embrace continuing education and professional development:

1. Attend workshops and conferences: Look for industry-specific workshops, conferences, and seminars. These events provide opportunities to learn from industry experts, participate in hands-on sessions, and network with like-minded professionals.

2. Enroll in online courses: Online platforms offer a wide range of courses on various topics, including business management, marketing, finance, and technology. Choose courses that align with your specific needs and goals and leverage the flexibility of online learning.

3. Seek mentorship and coaching: Find experienced mentors or coaches who can guide you based on their expertise and industry knowledge. They can provide insights, advice, and support as you navigate the challenges of running an online business.

4. Join professional associations and organizations: Join industry-specific associations or organizations that provide resources, networking opportunities, and access to educational resources. Engage in their events, forums, and publications to stay updated.

5. Read industry publications and books: Reading books, magazines, and online publications related to your industry helps expand your knowledge and keep you informed about industry trends, best practices, and thought leadership. Subscribe to relevant newsletters and follow industry blogs to receive regular updates.

6. Take advantage of online learning platforms: Platforms like Udemy, Coursera, LinkedIn Learning, and Skillshare offer a wide range of online courses and tutorials. Explore their course catalogs and choose topics that align with your interests and business needs.

7. Participate in webinars and podcasts: Webinars and podcasts are convenient ways to learn from industry experts and thought leaders. Look for relevant webinars and podcasts in your field and participate in live sessions or access recordings on-demand.

8. Set aside dedicated time for learning: Make continuous learning a priority by incorporating it into your schedule. Allocate regular time for reading industry publications, completing online courses, or engaging in other learning activities.

Remember that professional development is a lifelong

journey, and it's important to continually seek out opportunities for growth and improvement. By investing in your own education and development, you can stay ahead of the curve, ensure your skills remain relevant, and achieve long-term success as an online entrepreneur.

12.3 Embracing Change and Innovation

In the fast-paced world of online businesses, embracing change and innovation is crucial for staying relevant and maintaining a competitive edge. Here are the key reasons why you should embrace change and innovation, as well as strategies for doing so effectively:

Benefits of embracing change and innovation:

1. **Adaptability:** Embracing change allows you to quickly adapt to evolving customer needs, market trends, and technological advancements. This adaptability ensures your business can pivot and seize new opportunities as they arise.

2.   **Competitive   advantage:** Innovating and being open to change allows you to stay ahead of competitors. By constantly seeking ways to improve your products, services, and business processes, you can offer unique value to customers and stand out from the competition.

3.   **Growth   and   scalability:** Embracing change and innovation enables your business to grow and scale. By continually improving and expanding your offerings, you can attract new customers, increase revenue, and enter new markets.

4.   Customer   satisfaction: Adapting to changing customer preferences and needs leads to higher customer satisfaction. By innovating and offering new solutions or experiences, you can better meet customer expectations and build stronger customer relationships.

5. Continued relevance: The online business landscape is constantly evolving, and consumer preferences shift. By embracing change and innovation, you can ensure that your business remains relevant and doesn't become outdated or obsolete.

Strategies for embracing change and innovation:

1. Foster a culture of innovation: Encourage a culture within your business that promotes innovation and embraces change. Encourage employees to share their ideas, provide opportunities for brainstorming and collaboration, and reward creativity and risk-taking.

2. Stay informed about industry trends: Continuously monitor industry trends, market research, and customer feedback to identify potential areas for improvement and innovation. Stay updated on emerging technologies, changing consumer behaviors, and market disruptions that could impact your business.

3. Experiment and iterate: Be willing to experiment with new ideas, products, or strategies. Test different approaches, gather data, and iterate based on feedback and insights. Embrace a mentality of continuous improvement and learn from failures and successes alike.

4. Encourage customer feedback:
Regularly seek feedback from your customers to understand their changing needs and pain points. Use this feedback to make informed decisions about product enhancements, customer experience improvements, and other innovations.

5. Embrace technology advancements: Stay informed about technological advancements that can benefit your business. Be open to adopting new tools, software, automation, and other technologies that can streamline processes, improve efficiency, and enhance customer experiences.

6. Collaborate and network: Collaborate with other businesses, experts, and professionals in your industry to exchange ideas, share knowledge, and foster innovation. Participate in industry events, attend networking events, and actively engage in collaboration opportunities.

7. Encourage learning and professional development:

Provide opportunities for your team to learn and grow, whether through training programs, workshops, or online courses. Encourage them to stay updated on industry trends and technologies, and allocate resources for their professional development.

8. Embrace a mindset of continuous improvement: Cultivate a mindset of constantly seeking ways to improve and innovate. Encourage a proactive approach to reviewing and refining your business processes, products, and strategies on an ongoing basis.

Embracing change and innovation requires a willingness to step out of your comfort zone, take calculated risks, and continuously seek new opportunities. By remaining agile and adaptable, you can position your online business for long-term success in a rapidly evolving digital landscape.

CONCLUSION:

Starting and growing an online business can be an exciting and challenging journey. This book has provided a comprehensive guide to help you navigate this path, from understanding the reasons to start an online business to effectively scaling and innovating your operations.

Throughout the chapters, we explored various aspects of online entrepreneurship, including finding your niche, building your brand, setting up your online store, creating compelling content, driving traffic to your website, building an email list, providing excellent customer service, analyzing data, and making data-driven decisions, scaling your business, and considering legal and financial obligations.

It is essential to constantly adapt to industry trends and technologies, embrace change and innovation, and prioritize continuous learning and professional development. By leveraging the resources and tools recommended in the appendix, you can optimize your business operations and stay ahead in the competitive online landscape.

Remember, success in the online business world requires commitment, perseverance, and a strong understanding of your target market and their needs. By implementing the strategies and principles outlined in this book, you can build a thriving online business, create memorable customer experiences, and achieve your entrepreneurial goals.

So, go ahead and take the plunge into the world of online entrepreneurship. With dedication, strategic thinking, and a willingness to learn and adapt, you can turn your online business into a lucrative venture and make a lasting impact in your industry. Good luck on your entrepreneurial journey!

Appendix: Resources and Tools for Online Entrepreneurs

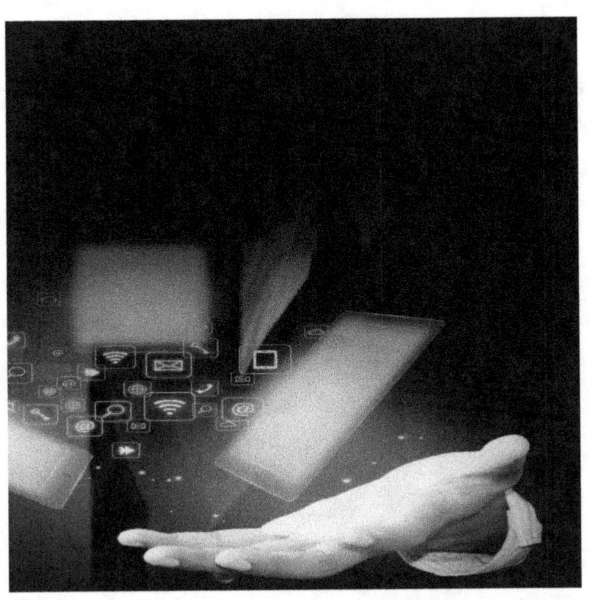

Below are some recommended resources and tools to help online entrepreneurs navigate their journey:

1. Website and E-commerce Platforms:

- Shopify: A popular and user-friendly e-commerce platform that allows you to build and customize your online store.

- **WordPress:** A versatile and widely-used website and blogging platform that offers e-commerce functionality through plugins like WooCommerce.

2. Market Research Tools:

- **Google Trends:** Provides insights into trending topics and search interest over time.

- **SEMRush:** Offers keyword research, competitive analysis, and SEO insights for your online business.

3. Customer Relationship Management (CRM) Software:

- **HubSpot CRM:** A comprehensive CRM platform that helps you manage customer information, track interactions, and automate marketing campaigns.

- **Salesforce:** A leading CRM platform that offers a range of tools for sales, marketing, and customer service.

4. Content Creation Tools:

- **Canva:** A versatile graphic design tool that allows you to create professional visuals and graphics for your online business.

- **Grammarly:** An AI-powered writing assistant that helps improve your writing and catch grammatical errors.

5. Email Marketing Platforms:

- **Mailchimp:** An intuitive email marketing platform that allows you to create and send professional email campaigns, manage subscriber lists, and track performance.

- **ConvertKit:** A powerful email marketing platform designed for creators and bloggers, with features like automation and segmentation.

6. Analytics and Tracking Tools:

- **Google Analytics:** A free web analytics tool that provides valuable information about your website's audience, traffic sources, and user behavior.

- **Hotjar:** A heatmapping and user feedback tool that helps you understand how visitors interact with your website.

7. Social Media Management Tools:

- **Hootsuite:** A social media management platform that allows you to schedule and manage your social media posts across multiple networks.

- **Buffer:** A social media scheduling and analytics tool that helps you streamline your social media marketing efforts.

8. Project Management Tools:

- **Trello:** A visual project management tool that helps you organize and prioritize tasks, collaborate with team members, and track progress.

- **Asana:** A flexible project management tool with features like task assignments, timelines, and integrations with other productivity tools.

Remember to assess your specific needs and requirements before selecting any tools or resources for your online business. Additionally, staying updated on emerging tools and technologies within your industry can help you stay ahead of the curve and optimize your business operations.

ROBERT JAY SAKI

www.ingramcontent.com/pod-product-compliance
Lightning Source LLC
Chambersburg PA
CBHW060038260726
48658CB00004B/1104